Crème Brûlée

Lou Seibert Pappas

Photographs by Alison Miksch

CHRONICLE BOOKS
SAN FRANCISCO

The Chronicle Books LLC edition published in 2009.

Text copyright © 2005 by Lou Seibert Pappas. Photographs copyright © 2005 by Alison Miksch. All rights reserved. No part of this book may be reproduced in any form without written permission from the publisher.

ISBN 978-0-8118-6682-8

The Library of Congress has cataloged the previous edition as follows:

Pappas, Lou Seibert.
    Crème Brûlée / by Lou Seibert Pappas ; photographs by Alison Miksch.
    --1st ed.
      p. cm.
    Includes index.
    ISBN 0-8118-4822-1 (hardcover)
    1.Puddings. 2. Desserts. I. Title.
TX773.P273 2005
641.8′ 644—dc22
                                    2004027698

Manufactured in China.

Design and Typesetting by Carole Goodman /
    Blue Anchor Design
Food styling by Jee Levin
Prop styling by Barbara Fritz
Photography assistance by Jada Vogt

10 9 8 7 6 5 4 3 2 1

Chronicle Books LLC
680 Second Street
San Francisco, California 94107

www.chroniclebooks.com

Callebaut is a registered trademark of S.A. Jacobs Suchard-Cote d'Or N.V.; Cointreau is a registered trademark of Cointreau Corporation; Frangelico is a registered trademark of C&C International Limited; Grand Marnier is a registered trademark of Société des Produits Marnier-Lapostolle; Guittard is a registered trademark of Guittard Chocolate Company; Ibarra is a registered trademark of Chocolatería de Jalisco, S. A. de C.V.; Kahlúa is a registered trademark of The Kahlúa Company; Lindt is a registered trademark of Chocoladefabriken Lindt &Sprüngli AG; Nutella is a registered trademark of Ferrero S.p.A.; Scharffen Berger is a registered trademark of SVS Chocolate LLC.; Valrhona is a registered trademark of Valrhona S.A.

There is no love sincerer than the love of food.

—GEORGE BERNARD SHAW

TABLE OF CONTENTS

CHOCOLATE AND NUTTY 57

SAVORY 76

INDEX 94

TABLE OF EQUIVALENTS 96

INTRODUCTION

WITH ITS SILKEN CUSTARD AND CARAMELIZED CRISP TOPPING, crème brûlée ranks as one of the most popular desserts in America. Around the globe, its innovative presence brings gustatory delight and pleasure galore as well.

The joys and rewards of making crème brûlée are multifold: It is quick and easy for a novice to prepare. It requires just four ingredients plus flavorings. It is elegant, luxurious, and versatile for countless dining occasions. And though its forte is mainly as a dessert, it has spawned tempting savory versions to enjoy around the clock. Savory custards can be served as first courses, side dishes, or light entrées. They may be topped with cheese, bread cubes, or, for a sweet touch, a light sprinkling of sugar.

Its roots can be traced to a recipe called Grilled Cream in a seventeenth-century English cookery book. It was first popularized in the dining halls at King's College in Cambridge. The close Spanish relative is *crema catalana,* a custard imbued with lemon and cinnamon. Though they have given the dish its name, it was only in recent years that the French acquired the custom of serving crème brûlée—or "burnt cream." (Both Escoffier's *Guide Culinaire* and *Larousse Gastronomique* bypass the subject.)

The preparation is a short two-part procedure. First, the rich custard mixture is prepared and baked. Sweet versions are then chilled, while savory ones are ready immediately. Then the top is caramelized. A butane gas blow-torch with a powerful approximately 2700 °F flame neatly browns the surface without reheating the custard or its container. By contrast, a broiler readily sears a battery of dishes at once and also warms the contents.

For the cook, the roster of flavors is boundless. Aromatic spices and fresh or dried herbs—lavender, basil, ginger, lemongrass, chiles, and kaffir lime leaves—can scent these custards. Various liqueurs and liquors, Mexican chocolate, and a bevy of sugars lend intrigue.

As your family and guests tap through the caramel-sealed top to relish the rich, velvety interior of these custards, compliments will abound. This collection of tantalizing recipes offers taste-tingling surprise and delight.

Enjoy!

—*Lou Seibert Pappas*

INGREDIENTS

Cream: The classic cream for crème brûlée is heavy (whipping) cream, containing 36 percent butterfat and readily available in half-pint and 1-pint containers in grocery stores. It contains the proper amount of butterfat. When you add rich ingredients, such as cheeses in savory recipes or chocolate in dessert recipes, you may choose to lighten the fat content by replacing some of the heavy cream with half-and-half (10.5 percent butterfat) or light cream (18 percent). The substitution of all half-and-half or milk for the cream results in a dish similar to a regular baked egg custard rather than a rich crème brûlée.

Sugar: For sweetening the custard, fine granulated or light brown sugar is usually the preferred choice. For caramelizing the top, many options abound: superfine sugar, regular granulated sugar, confectioners' sugar, light or dark brown sugar, or raw sugar such as demerara or turbinado. Shaved piloncillo, a Mexican brown sugar, yields a delectable molasses-style topping.

Eggs: Grade-A large eggs are the traditional choice for recipes and were used in testing. It is important to keep eggs refrigerated and to check the date on the carton to ensure freshness. The proportions used in this book are 6 egg yolks to 2 cups of cream. When rich ingredients such as chocolate and cheese are added, the number of yolks is sometimes reduced.

Flavorings: Vanilla beans, with their tiny black flavor-packed seeds, lend more flavor than vanilla extract when vanilla is the primary flavoring, yet pure vanilla extract is a desirable complementary addition to other flavorings in many recipes. Liquors and liqueurs are superb enhancers. Choices include brandy, Cognac, Calvados, dark rum, tequila, and liqueurs such as Grand Marnier, Triple Sec, Kahlúa, amaretto, framboise, and Poire William.

Herbs and Spices: Lavender, lemongrass, ginger, kaffir lime leaves, basil, chives, tarragon, and dill lend a special touch to sweet and savory crèmes brûlées.

Fruit: Practically any fruit can be used in a crème brûlée, with the exception of pineapple. Fresh pineapple contains an enzyme that prevents a custard from setting properly. Fruits at the peak of their season are the most flavorful.

Chocolate: White chocolate, milk chocolate, bittersweet, or semisweet chocolate are incorporated into some crèmes brûlées. Choose a fine-quality bittersweet chocolate containing a high proportion of cocoa butter and pure chocolate. Among the desirable brands are Callebaut, Scharffen Berger, Lindt, Guittard, and Valrhona.

Savory Ingredients: A variety of cheeses, vegetables, herbs, and seafood enhance savory custards. Some of the custards in this book are more like savory bread puddings.

EQUIPMENT

Baking Dishes: Many styles of ovenproof baking dishes are available, but the standard size is a 5-inch-diameter flan dish (measured across the top). A 6-ounce porcelain ramekin (a miniature soufflé dish) can be substituted for the flan dishes called for in these recipes. And even a slightly smaller 5¼-ounce ramekin can accommodate, although you may want to slightly decrease the amount of sugar or cheese used for topping. (See Caramelizing the Sugar and Browning the Cheese on page 11.) Other styles such as square or heart-shaped dishes are sometimes used in fine restaurants. If you prefer a generous sugar crust, choose dishes with a larger surface. Any ovenproof dish can also be used, such as custard cups or small baking dishes.

Bain-Marie: A large baking pan or roasting pan should be used as a bain-marie, or water bath, during baking. Place the prepared dishes in the pan and fill it with warm water to come halfway up the sides of the dishes. This provides even, gentle moist heat.

Whisk: A balloon-type stainless-steel wire whisk is handy for beating eggs swiftly and easily.

Grater and Zester: For zesting citrus, a grater or zester is invaluable for making fine shreds of zest.

Double Boiler: A double boiler is composed of two pans that fit together; water is heated in the lower pan. The water should be held at a simmering point and be at least 1 inch below the surface of the top pan. This pan is useful for melting chocolate and cooking delicate foods such as custards and egg dishes, to prevent them from overheating or curdling. To improvise this pan, place a stainless-steel bowl over a saucepan filled with 1 inch of barely simmering water.

Sieve: A sieve, or strainer, is useful for removing solid flavorings such as herbs and spices from hot cream or sauces. Purists may strain custard before baking to remove fine particles such as citrus zest or egg threads. A small sieve is best to use for evenly dusting confectioners' sugar; just stir it with a spoon while moving the sieve above the dessert.

Butane Blowtorch: A hand-powered butane blowtorch is the ideal tool for caramelizing a sugar topping (or browning a cheese topping) swiftly and efficiently. It quickly sears sugar within a minute without overheating the container. Follow the manufacturer's instructions for use.

Broiler: An alternative to the torch is an oven broiler. It heats the dishes during broiling, making them too hot to serve, so sweet custards will need a brief refrigeration of 5 minutes before serving. (It is desirable to serve savory custards piping hot.) Broiling does have the advantage of finishing many custards simultaneously, but care must be taken to avoid burning the sugar.

Salamander: This tool, available in some kitchen shops, consists of a metal disk with a long handle; the disk is heated over a gas flame and then placed directly on the sugar to caramelize it, much like a branding iron.

TECHNIQUES

IF YOU CHECK A DOZEN COOKBOOKS FOR CRÈME BRÛLÉE
recipes, you are likely to find a dozen different methods for assembling and baking the custards. This is surprising, given the few ingredients involved.

Many recipes advise scalding or boiling the cream and baking the custard at a temperature as high as 350°F. Yet culinary science tells us that the best results are obtained when eggs are heated slowly and gently. *Cook's Illustrated* magazine tested thirty-six methods for making crème brûlée, and my testing collaborated their results. Luckily, the simplest method—using cold ingredients and low heat—proved the best.

The cream does not need heating and is best used directly from the refrigerator or cooled to room temperature if it was heated with flavorings. Some recipes say to cook the cream-egg mixture in a double boiler, but this stove-top method heats the mixture too quickly for it to thicken the liquid properly and yields a soft, runny custard. A baking temperature of 275°F yields a silkier product than does a higher temperature. You can check for doneness by looking to see if the center of each custard still jiggles slightly.

PREPARING THE CUSTARD

Cold eggs are easier to separate, because the yolks are firmer. If you plan to use the egg whites in a soufflé or cake, use three dishes when separating eggs, as a speck of yolk in the whites prevents them from beating to maximum volume.

Whisk the cream into the beaten yolks without overbeating, as bubbles are not desirable.

If melting chocolate to add to the custard, melt it over barely simmering water to keep from overheating it, as it can scorch easily.

Pour the mixture into the dishes, allowing at least ¼ inch head space for the sugar topping.

A baked custard is done when the center still jiggles slightly, as it will continue to firm up once it is removed from the oven.

CHILLING

Sweet custards should be refrigerated for at least 2 hours, or up to 2 days, before caramelizing.

CARAMELIZING THE SUGAR

Different sugars produce slightly different results when caramelized. Brown sugar tends to melt the quickest, in less than a minute. Superfine and regular granulated sugar melt to form a thin, solid disk. Confectioners' sugar should be sifted or pressed through a sieve to make an even layer so it will brown evenly. Raw sugars are slower to melt than finer sugars, but produce a nice, even browning.

Oven-Dried Brown Sugar: Due to the moisture content of brown sugar, it is recommended to dry it before caramelizing. Spread light or dark brown sugar out on a baking sheet in a ⅛-inch layer and bake in a preheated 275 °F oven for 8 to 10 minutes, or until browned a shade darker. Let cool, place in a small resealable plastic bag, and crush it thoroughly with a rolling pin or flat metal mallet to make fine crystals. Brown sugar treated in this manner has an excellent flavor when caramelized.

The amount of sugar you use to caramelize the top can vary with personal taste and the diameter of the dish. If you use flan dishes, which have a wider diameter, 1 tablespoon of sugar is a good amount for each dish. With a 6-ounce or smaller ramekin, which has a 4-inch or less diameter, about 2 teaspoons of sugar will cover the surface nicely.

When caramelizing the sugar topping of dessert crèmes brûlées under a broiler, you may prefer to place the containers in a pan and fill the pan with cold water and ice to come halfway up the sides of the dishes. This keeps the containers from overheating, and you can serve the desserts immediately (rather than refrigerating them briefly to cool).

BROWNING THE CHEESE

The blowtorch technique for browning cheese is essentially the same as that used to caramelize sugar (see below). For savory recipes that call for cheese toppings, use 4 teaspoons grated Parmesan cheese for each flan dish or about 3 teaspoons if substituting ramekin-size dishes.

USING A BLOWTORCH OR A BROILER

Use caution and follow the manufacturer's instructions when using a blowtorch. Searing one dish at a time, hold the blowtorch about 4 inches from the top of the dish, moving the torch constantly so that the sugar (or cheese) browns evenly. Be especially careful if the custard contains alcohol, as it can cause the sugar to sputter. When using a broiler to caramelize, place the dishes about 4 inches from the heat source. Watch carefully and turn the baking sheet holding the dishes if necessary to brown the custards evenly. Wear oven mitts when broiling and handling the baking sheet in the oven.

Sugar disks can be made separately from the custard. Place a sheet of aluminum foil on a baking pan. Place a 5- or 4-inch-diameter bowl upside down on the foil and draw around it with a pencil; use the larger size for flan dishes and the smaller size for ramekins. Repeat as needed to make the disks. Spread vegetable oil or unsalted butter lightly over each circle. Sprinkle 1 tablespoon of raw or oven-dried brown sugar or granulated sugar evenly over the circle for flan-size custards, or 2 teaspoons for ramekin-size ones. Using a hand-held blowtorch, caramelize the sugar by holding the torch about 4 inches from the surface of the foil and moving the torch to brown the sugar evenly. Or, preheat the broiler and place under the broiler 4 inches from the heat source; watching carefully, broil until the sugar caramelizes, 1 to 2 minutes. Let cool, then remove by peeling off the foil. Store in an airtight container for up to 4 days.

Crème brûlée can be made up to 2 days in advance and refrigerated, but wait to add the sugar topping and caramelize it until shortly before serving. If you have used a broiler to caramelize, refrigerate the sweet crèmes brûlées for 5 minutes to cool the dishes slightly before serving. The topping will start to melt and liquefy after about 1 hour.

CLASSIC
AND CREATIVE

THIS CAPTIVATING COLLECTION COVERS A SPECTRUM OF flavors imbued with spices and herbs, liqueurs, and prominent holiday foods such as eggnog, cranberries, and pumpkin. The delectable sweets lend a perfect finale to a luncheon or dinner menu. Plus, they are ideal desserts to prepare in advance.

Classic Vanilla Bean Crème Brûlée

The classic crème brûlée has spawned countless flavor variations, yet this refined version is elegant in its simplicity. A vanilla bean is a must for superb flavor; vanilla extract is not an equal substitute.

SERVES 6

2 cups heavy (whipping) cream

4-inch piece vanilla bean, split lengthwise

6 large egg yolks

⅓ cup granulated sugar

2 tablespoons Cognac (optional)

6 tablespoons oven-dried brown sugar (see page 11) or granulated sugar for topping

Pour the cream into a medium saucepan, scrape the seeds from the vanilla bean into the cream, and add the vanilla pod. Place over medium heat until small bubbles form around the edges of the pan. Remove from the heat and let cool to room temperature. Remove the vanilla pod and scrape any remaining seeds into the cream.

Preheat the oven to 275 °F.

In a medium bowl, whisk the egg yolks until pale in color. Whisk in the ⅓ cup granulated sugar until dissolved. Gradually whisk in the cream. Stir in the Cognac, if desired.

Place six standard-size flan dishes in a baking pan. Divide the custard mixture among the dishes. Pour warm water into the pan to come halfway up the sides of the dishes. Bake in the oven for 35 to 40 minutes, or until the center of each custard still jiggles slightly. Remove from the oven and lift the dishes from the hot water. Let cool briefly, then refrigerate for at least 2 hours or up to 2 days.

When ready to serve, place the dishes on a baking sheet. Evenly sprinkle 1 tablespoon brown or granulated sugar over each custard. Using a hand-held blowtorch, caramelize the sugar (see page 11).

Catalan Cinnamon Crème Brûlée

In Spain, this is called *crema catalana* (Catalonian cream) or *crema cremada*, "burnt cream." The Catalans claim to have invented the custard, though its roots are traced to a seventeenth-century English recipe. Sometimes, Spanish restaurants serve it without the caramelized sugar topping. If your herb garden boasts lemon balm, garnish each dish with a sprig to exude a citrus aroma.

SERVES 6

1 ½ cups heavy (whipping) cream

½ cup half-and-half

1 cinnamon stick

¼ teaspoon freshly grated nutmeg

2 tablespoons grated lemon zest

6 large egg yolks

⅓ cup sugar, plus 6 tablespoons for topping

Lemon wedges for garnish

Lemon balm or mint sprigs for garnish (optional)

Preheat the oven to 275 °F. In a medium saucepan, combine the cream, half-and-half, cinnamon stick, nutmeg, and lemon zest. Place over medium heat until small bubbles form around the edges of the pan. Remove from the heat and let cool to room temperature. Remove the cinnamon stick.

In a medium bowl, whisk the egg yolks until pale in color, then whisk in the ⅓ cup sugar until dissolved. Whisk in the cream mixture.

Place six standard-size flan dishes in a baking pan. Divide the custard mixture among the dishes. Pour warm water into the pan to come halfway up the sides of the dishes. Bake in the oven for 35 to 40 minutes, or until the center of each custard still jiggles slightly. Remove from the oven and lift the dishes from the hot water. Let cool briefly, then refrigerate for at least 2 hours or up to 2 days.

When ready to serve, place the dishes on a baking sheet and evenly sprinkle 1 tablespoon sugar over each custard. Using a hand-held blowtorch, caramelize the sugar (see page 11). Garnish each dish with a lemon wedge and a sprig of lemon balm or mint, if desired.

Cappuccino Crème Brûlée

Here's a crème brûlée with a rich coffee flavor, accented by Kahlúa or brandy. It is nice to garnish the top with a few chocolate-covered coffee beans. Turbinado sugar is a raw sugar with coarse blond crystals and a delicate molasses flavor.

SERVES 6

5 teaspoons instant espresso or instant coffee granules

2 tablespoons hot water

2 cups heavy (whipping) cream

6 large egg yolks

⅓ cup firmly packed light brown sugar

3 tablespoons Kahlúa or brandy

6 tablespoons oven-dried brown sugar (see page 11) or turbinado sugar for topping

Preheat the oven to 275 °F. In a medium bowl, dissolve the espresso or coffee granules in the hot water and stir in the cream.

In another medium bowl, whisk the egg yolks until pale in color. Whisk in the light brown sugar until dissolved. Whisk in the espresso mixture and the Kahlúa or brandy.

Place six standard-size flan dishes in a baking pan. Divide the custard mixture among the dishes. Pour warm water into the pan to come halfway up the sides of the dishes. Bake in the oven for 35 to 40 minutes, or until the center of each custard still jiggles slightly. Remove from the oven and lift the dishes from the hot water. Let cool briefly, then refrigerate for at least 2 hours or up to 2 days.

When ready to serve, place the dishes on a baking sheet and evenly sprinkle 1 tablespoon oven-dried brown or turbinado sugar over each custard. Using a hand-held blowtorch, caramelize the sugar (see page 11).

Crème Brûlée à l'Orange

This ultrapopular rich custard dessert is elegant unadorned, yet it lends itself to sumptuous embellishments, such as a shower of fresh raspberries, blackberries, sliced strawberries, or blueberries. Or, add a frosty fillip with a dollop of vanilla bean ice cream or toasted almond ice cream.

SERVES 6

6 large egg yolks

⅓ cup sugar, plus 6 tablespoons for topping

2 cups heavy (whipping) cream

2 teaspoons grated orange zest

3 tablespoons Grand Marnier, curaçao, or other orange liqueur

Preheat the oven to 275 °F. In a medium bowl, whisk the egg yolks until pale in color and then whisk in the ⅓ cup sugar until dissolved. Whisk in the cream, orange zest, and orange liqueur.

Place six standard-size flan dishes in a baking pan. Divide the custard mixture among the dishes. Pour warm water into the pan to come halfway up the sides of the dishes. Bake in the oven for 35 to 40 minutes, or until the center of each custard still jiggles slightly. Remove from the oven and lift the dishes from the hot water. Let cool briefly, then refrigerate for at least 2 hours or up to 2 days.

When ready to serve, place the dishes on a baking sheet and evenly sprinkle 1 tablespoon sugar over each custard. Using a hand-held blowtorch, caramelize the sugar (see page 11).

Eggnog Crème Brûlée

Perfect for the holidays, this rich custard is an ideal finish to a gala family or guest dinner. Enlist any young guests to help with the last-minute touch of sprinkling the sugar over the custards before caramelizing; they enjoy having a part in the cooking procedure. Freshly grated nutmeg adds incomparable flavor.

SERVES 6

6 large egg yolks

⅓ cup granulated sugar

2 cups heavy (whipping) cream

½ teaspoon freshly grated nutmeg

2 tablespoons brandy

2 tablespoons rum

6 tablespoons oven-dried brown
   sugar (see page 11) for topping

Preheat the oven to 275°F. In a medium bowl, whisk the egg yolks until pale in color, then whisk in the granulated sugar until dissolved. Whisk in the cream, nutmeg, brandy, and rum.

Place six standard-size flan dishes in a baking pan. Divide the custard mixture among the dishes. Pour warm water into the pan to come halfway up the sides of the dishes. Bake in the oven for 35 to 40 minutes, or until the center of each custard still jiggles slightly. Remove from the oven and lift the dishes from the hot water. Let cool briefly, then refrigerate for at least 2 hours or up to 2 days.

When ready to serve, place the dishes on a baking sheet and evenly sprinkle 1 tablespoon brown sugar over each custard. Using a hand-held blowtorch, caramelize the sugar (see page 11).

Lavender-Lemon Crème Brûlée

Fresh or dried lavender flowers imbue a classic crème brûlée with their intriguing scent. Choose French lavender, as it has a pleasing, decisive flavor, while other varieties can have a medicinal overtone. Garnish with lavender blossoms to identify the dish.

SERVES 6

2 cups heavy (whipping) cream

2 tablespoons fresh or 1 ½ teaspoons dried lavender blossoms, plus more for garnish

2 teaspoons grated lemon zest

6 large egg yolks

⅓ cup granulated sugar

6 tablespoons confectioners' sugar, sifted, for topping

Preheat the oven to 275 °F. In a medium saucepan, combine the cream, lavender blossoms, and the lemon zest. Place over medium heat until small bubbles form around the edges of the pan. Remove from the heat and let cool to room temperature. Strain through a sieve and discard the lavender.

In a medium bowl, whisk the egg yolks until pale in color. Whisk in the granulated sugar until dissolved. Whisk in the lavender-flavored cream.

Place six standard-size flan dishes in a baking pan. Divide the custard mixture among the dishes. Pour warm water into the pan to come halfway up the sides of the dishes. Bake in the oven for 35 to 40 minutes, or until the center of each custard still jiggles slightly. Remove from the oven and lift the dishes from the hot water. Let cool briefly, then refrigerate for at least 2 hours or up to 2 days.

When ready to serve, place the dishes on a baking sheet and, using a small sieve, evenly sprinkle 1 tablespoon confectioners' sugar over each custard. Using a hand-held blowtorch, caramelize the sugar (see page 11). Garnish each dish with a few lavender blossoms.

Thai-Style Lemongrass Crème Brûlée

Alan Wong's Restaurant in Honolulu offers diners five Chinese porcelain soup spoons, each filled with a different flavor of crème brûlée for a dazzling presentation and a taste-tingling teaser. This is a takeoff on his Thai flavor. The kaffir lime leaves, lemongrass, and ginger make such an exotic flavor combo that the chile addition is optional.

SERVES 6

2 cups heavy (whipping) cream

1 stalk lemongrass, white part only, peeled

1-inch piece fresh ginger, peeled and chopped (about 3 tablespoons)

6 kaffir lime leaves

1 Thai (bird) chile, halved (optional)

6 large egg yolks

⅓ cup granulated sugar

2 tablespoons Cognac (optional)

6 tablespoons oven-dried brown sugar (see page 11) or raw sugar for topping

Edible blossoms such as nasturtiums for garnish (optional)

Preheat the oven to 275 °F. In a medium saucepan, combine the cream, lemongrass, ginger, lime leaves, and optional chile. Place over medium heat until small bubbles form around the edges of the pan. Remove from the heat and let cool to room temperature. Strain through a sieve and discard the lemongrass, ginger, lime leaves, and chile.

In a medium bowl, whisk the egg yolks until pale in color and whisk in the granulated sugar until dissolved. Whisk in the flavored cream and Cognac, if desired.

Place six standard-size flan dishes in a baking pan. Divide the custard mixture among the dishes. Pour warm water into the pan to come halfway up the sides of the dishes. Bake in the oven for 35 to 40 minutes, or until the center of each custard still jiggles slightly. Remove from the oven and lift the dishes from the hot water. Let cool briefly, then refrigerate for at least 2 hours or up to 2 days.

When ready to serve, place the dishes on a baking sheet and evenly sprinkle 1 tablespoon brown or raw sugar over each custard. Using a hand-held blowtorch, caramelize the sugar (see page 11).

Margarita Crème Brûlée

The juicy flesh of mango or golden kiwi fruit accents this delightful cocktail-styled dessert. As an option, papaya may replace the mango.

SERVES 6

6 large egg yolks

⅓ cup granulated sugar

2 cups heavy (whipping) cream

6 tablespoons tequila

2 tablespoons curaçao, Cointreau, or Triple Sec

3 tablespoons freshly squeezed lime juice

1 tablespoon grated orange zest

6 tablespoons confectioners' sugar for topping

1 mango, peeled, pitted, and diced or 3 golden kiwi fruit, peeled and diced for serving

Preheat the oven to 275°F. In a medium bowl, whisk the egg yolks until pale in color. Whisk in the granulated sugar until dissolved. Whisk in the cream, tequila, orange liqueur, lime juice, and orange zest.

Place six standard-size flan dishes in a baking pan. Divide the custard mixture among the dishes. Pour warm water into the pan to come halfway up the sides of the dishes. Bake in the oven for 35 to 40 minutes, or until the center of each custard still jiggles slightly. Remove from the oven and lift the dishes from the hot water. Let cool briefly, then refrigerate for at least 2 hours or up to 2 days.

When ready to serve, place the dishes on a baking sheet and, using a small sieve, evenly sprinkle 1 tablespoon confectioners' sugar over each custard. Using a hand-held blowtorch, caramelize the sugar (see page 11). Serve on dessert plates, with the mango or kiwi fruit alongside.

Crystallized Ginger Crème Brûlée

Fresh ginger plus crystallized ginger lends a double boost of hot sweetness to this creamy dessert.

SERVES 6

2 cups heavy (whipping) cream

3 tablespoons chopped peeled
fresh ginger

6 large egg yolks

⅓ cup granulated sugar

¼ cup finely chopped crystallized
ginger

1 teaspoon vanilla extract

TROPICAL FRUIT SALAD:

2 kiwi fruit (about 6 ounces total),
green and gold if possible

1½ cups diced fresh pineapple

1½ cups diced fresh mango

3 tablespoons Grand Marnier,
curaçao, or other orange
liqueur (optional)

6 tablespoons oven-dried brown
sugar (see page 11) for topping

Preheat the oven to 275°F. In a medium saucepan, combine the cream and fresh ginger. Place over medium heat until small bubbles form around the edges of the pan. Remove from the heat and let cool to room temperature. Strain through a sieve, discarding the ginger.

In a medium bowl, whisk the egg yolks until pale in color. Whisk in the granulated sugar until dissolved. Whisk in the flavored cream and stir in the crystallized ginger and vanilla extract.

Place six standard-size flan dishes in a baking pan. Divide the custard mixture among the dishes. Pour warm water into the pan to come halfway up the sides of the dishes. Bake in the oven for 35 to 40 minutes, or until the center of each custard still jiggles slightly. Remove from the oven and lift the dishes from the hot water. Let cool briefly, then refrigerate for at least 2 hours or up to 2 days.

To make the fruit salad: In a large bowl, toss the kiwi fruit, pineapple, and mango. Sprinkle with the orange liqueur, if desired. Refrigerate, covered, until serving time or up to 1 day.

When ready to serve, place the flan dishes on a baking sheet and evenly sprinkle 1 tablespoon brown sugar over each custard. Using a hand-held blowtorch, caramelize the sugar (see page 11).

Spicy Pumpkin Crème Brûlée

This is an ideal dessert for the Thanksgiving holiday dinner and a nice switch on the traditional pumpkin pie. The custards can be baked well in advance, ready for a last-minute caramelizing. If teenagers are present, they will enjoy the task of sprinkling on the sugar topping and watching it caramelize.

SERVES 6

6 tablespoons chopped raw almonds or pecans, toasted (see note)

6 large egg yolks

½ cup firmly packed light brown sugar

¾ cup puréed cooked pumpkin or butternut squash

½ cup sour cream

1 ¼ cups heavy (whipping) cream

1 teaspoon ground cinnamon

½ teaspoon ground ginger

¼ teaspoon Chinese five-spice powder

6 tablespoons oven-dried brown sugar (see page 11) or raw sugar for topping

Have ready the toasted nuts. Preheat the oven to 275°F. In a medium bowl, whisk the egg yolks until pale in color. Whisk in the ½ cup light brown sugar until dissolved. Whisk in the pumpkin, sour cream, heavy cream, cinnamon, ginger, and five-spice powder.

Place six standard-size flan dishes in a baking pan. Divide the custard mixture among the dishes. Sprinkle with the nuts. Pour warm water into the pan to come halfway up the sides of the dishes. Bake in the oven for 35 to 40 minutes, or until the center of each custard still jiggles slightly. Remove from the oven and lift the dishes from the hot water. Let cool briefly, then refrigerate for at least 2 hours or up to 2 days.

When ready to serve, place the dishes on a baking sheet and evenly sprinkle 1 tablespoon oven-dried brown sugar or raw sugar over each custard. Using a hand-held blowtorch, caramelize the sugar (see page 11).

Toasting Nuts: Preheat the oven to 325°F. Spread the nuts on a rimmed baking sheet and bake in the oven for 8 to 10 minutes, or until toasted. Transfer the nuts to a bowl.

Cranberry-Orange Crème Brûlée

Dried cranberries add a tart-sweet bite and a holiday twist to this classic dessert. Muscat or golden raisins or dried cherries are nice in place of the dried cranberries another time.

SERVES 6

6 large egg yolks

⅓ cup granulated sugar

¼ cup thawed frozen orange juice concentrate

1¾ cups heavy (whipping) cream

¼ teaspoon ground cloves

1 teaspoon vanilla extract

⅔ cup dried cranberries, dried cherries, golden raisins, or muscat raisins

6 tablespoons turbinado sugar for topping

Preheat the oven to 275 °F. In a medium bowl, whisk the egg yolks until pale in color and whisk in the granulated sugar until dissolved. Whisk in the orange juice, cream, cloves, vanilla extract, and cranberries or other dried fruit.

Place six standard-size flan dishes in a baking pan. Divide the custard mixture among the dishes. Pour warm water into the pan to come halfway up the sides of the dishes. Bake in the oven for 35 to 40 minutes, or until the center of each custard still jiggles slightly. Remove from the oven and lift the dishes from the hot water. Let cool briefly, then refrigerate for at least 2 hours or up to 2 days.

When ready to serve, place the dishes on a baking sheet and evenly sprinkle 1 tablespoon turbinado sugar over each custard. Using a hand-held blowtorch, caramelize the sugar (see page 11).

FRUITY
AND FABULOUS

THIS SAMPLING OF ENTICING FRUIT-ADORNED CRÈMES BRÛLÉES features a selection of fresh and dried fruits. The decorative dishes are accented by liquor, liqueurs, wine, and champagne. Several of the desserts are no-bake style. They utilize Greek yogurt or sour cream or rely on stove-top custard.

Blueberry-Brandy Crème Brûlée

Fresh blueberries jewel this rich sour cream custard for a sumptuous texture and flavor contrast.

SERVES 6

2 cups fresh or frozen blueberries

6 large egg yolks

⅓ cup sugar, plus 6 tablespoons for topping

½ cup sour cream

1½ cups heavy (whipping) cream

2 teaspoons grated lemon zest

2 tablespoons brandy or rum

Preheat the oven to 275 °F. Reserve ½ cup of the blueberries for garnish. Divide the remaining blueberries among six standard-size flan dishes.

In a medium bowl, whisk the egg yolks until pale in color and whisk in the ⅓ cup sugar until dissolved. Gradually whisk in the sour cream and heavy cream. Blend in the lemon zest and brandy or rum.

Place the dishes in a heavy baking pan. Divide the custard mixture among the dishes. Pour warm water into the pan to come halfway up the sides of the dishes. Bake in the oven for 35 to 40 minutes, or until the center of each custard still jiggles slightly. Remove from the oven and lift the dishes from the hot water. Let cool briefly, then refrigerate for at least 2 hours or up to 1 day.

When ready to serve, place the dishes on a baking sheet and evenly sprinkle 1 tablespoon sugar over each custard. Using a hand-held blowtorch, caramelize the sugar (see page 11). Garnish the top of each dish with the reserved blueberries.

Mango Crème Brûlée

The tropical taste of fresh mango permeates a creamy custard enhanced with a splash of rum and lime juice.

SERVES 6

¾ cup diced fresh mango

1¾ cups heavy (whipping) cream

6 large egg yolks

⅓ cup sugar, plus 6 tablespoons for topping

2 tablespoons dark rum

1 tablespoon freshly squeezed lime juice

Lime wedges for garnish

Preheat the oven to 275 °F. In a blender, purée the mango with ½ cup of the cream.

In a medium bowl, whisk the egg yolks until pale in color. Whisk in the ⅓ cup sugar until dissolved. Whisk in the mango purée, the remaining 1¼ cups cream, the rum, and lime juice.

Place six standard-size flan dishes in a baking pan. Divide the custard mixture among the dishes. Pour warm water into the pan to come halfway up the sides of the dishes. Bake in the oven for 35 to 40 minutes, or until the center of each custard still jiggles slightly. Remove from the oven and lift the dishes from the hot water. Let cool briefly, then refrigerate for 2 hours or up to 2 days.

When ready to serve, place the dishes on a baking sheet and evenly sprinkle 1 tablespoon sugar over each custard. Using a hand-held blowtorch, caramelize the sugar (see page 11). Serve each dish with a lime wedge.

Balsamic-Blackberry Crème Brûlée

Rich, thick Greek yogurt cloaks balsamic-scented blackberries for a refreshing, lower-fat brûlée.

SERVES 6

2 ½ cups fresh blackberries

3 tablespoons 5- to 10-year-old balsamic vinegar

1 ⅔ cups unflavored Greek yogurt or other whole-milk yogurt

⅓ cup sour cream

¼ cup orange blossom honey

6 tablespoons oven-dried brown sugar (see page 11) or turbinado sugar for topping

Put the blackberries in a small bowl and sprinkle with the vinegar. Let stand for 15 minutes. Reserve ½ cup of the berries for garnish. Divide the remaining berries among six standard-size flan dishes.

In a medium bowl, stir together the yogurt and sour cream and divide the mixture among the dishes. Drizzle with the honey. Refrigerate for 1 hour.

When ready to serve, place the dishes on a baking sheet and evenly sprinkle 1 tablespoon brown or turbinado sugar over each custard. Using a hand-held blowtorch, caramelize the sugar (see page 11). Garnish the top of each dish with the reserved blackberries.

Cherry Risotto Crème Brûlée

Old-fashioned rice pudding is elevated to three-star status in this creamy brûlée. Use Arborio or another short-grain Italian rice for the best texture. If fresh cherries are in season, let them stand in for the dried ones.

SERVES 6

⅓ cup dried cherries or 1½ cups fresh Bing cherries, pitted

4 tablespoons kirsch

2 cups whole milk

⅔ cup Arborio rice

1 cinnamon stick

⅓ cup sugar, plus 6 tablespoons for topping

5 large egg yolks

1½ cups heavy (whipping) cream

1 teaspoon vanilla extract (optional)

Preheat the oven to 325 °F. Put the cherries in a small bowl and add 2 tablespoons of the kirsch. Let stand for 15 minutes.

In a medium saucepan, combine the milk, rice, and cinnamon stick. Bring to a boil, and reduce the heat to medium-low. Cover and cook for 15 minutes, or until the rice is al dente and about ½ cup milk remains. Remove from the heat and stir in the ⅓ cup sugar. Let cool to room temperature.

In a medium bowl, whisk the egg yolks until pale in color. Whisk in the cream and the remaining 2 tablespoons kirsch or, alternatively, the vanilla extract. Stir in the rice mixture.

Place six standard-size flan dishes in a baking pan. Reserve a dozen cherries for garnish and divide the remainder among the dishes. Divide the custard mixture and any juices from the cherries among the dishes (discarding the cinnamon stick). Pour warm water into the pan to come halfway up the sides of the dishes. Bake in the oven for 35 to 40 minutes, or until the center of each custard still jiggles slightly. Remove from the oven and lift the dishes from the hot water. Let cool briefly, then refrigerate for at least 2 hours or up to 2 days.

When ready to serve, place the dishes on a baking sheet and evenly sprinkle 1 tablespoon sugar over each custard. Using a hand-held blowtorch, caramelize the sugar (see page 11). Garnish the top of each dish with a cherry or two.

Strawberry Zabaglione Crème Brûlée

Zabaglione studded with berries was a favorite of my Italian neighbor's, who decorated the dessert with whipped cream. Choose an elegant dessert wine to enhance this brûlée version of the stove-top custard.

SERVES 6

2½ cups fresh strawberries

6 large egg yolks

⅓ cup granulated sugar, plus 24 teaspoons for topping

1 teaspoon grated lemon zest

½ cup Malvasia Blanca or other dessert wine

1 cup heavy (whipping) cream

2 tablespoons framboise

Vegetable oil for brushing

1 tablespoon confectioners' sugar

Reserve 6 of the strawberries for garnish. Cut the remaining strawberries into slices. Divide the sliced strawberries among six standard-size flan dishes.

In the top of a double boiler, whisk the egg yolks with the ⅓ cup granulated sugar and lemon zest until blended. Place over simmering water and whisk until the yolks are light and foamy. Gradually whisk in the wine and ½ cup of the cream. Continue to whisk or beat with a hand-held electric mixer until the mixture is thick and light and triples in volume, about 15 minutes. Blend in 1 tablespoon of the framboise.

Divide the mixture among the dishes. Refrigerate for 1 hour.

Line a baking sheet with aluminum foil. Place a 5-inch-diameter bowl on the foil and draw around it; repeat to make 6 circles. Brush the circles with vegetable oil. Evenly sprinkle each circle with 4 teaspoons sugar, covering the circles completely. Using a hand-held blowtorch, caramelize the sugar (see page 11). Let cool for a few minutes, then carefully peel the caramel disks from the foil.

In a deep bowl, whip the remaining ½ cup cream until soft peaks form. Blend in the confectioners' sugar and the remaining 1 tablespoon framboise.

When ready to serve, cut each of the reserved strawberries into wedges, leaving them attached at the end, and spread open to resemble a flower. Place a caramel disk on top of each dish. Garnish with flavored whipped cream and a cut strawberry.

Berry Patch Crème Brûlée

A medley of berries gives a juicy flavor-packed taste to every biteful of this creamy dessert. A touch of framboise lends a delicious uplift.

SERVES 6

2½ cups mixed fresh blueberries, raspberries, and blackberries

6 large egg yolks

⅓ cup sugar, plus 6 tablespoons for topping

⅓ cup mascarpone or sour cream

1⅔ cups heavy (whipping) cream

2 tablespoons framboise

Preheat the oven to 275 °F. Reserve ½ cup of the berries for garnish. Place six standard-size flan dishes in a baking pan. Divide the remaining berries among the dishes.

In a medium bowl, whisk the egg yolks until pale in color. Whisk in the ⅓ cup sugar until dissolved. Whisk in the mascarpone or sour cream, then gradually whisk in the heavy cream. Stir in the framboise.

Divide the custard mixture among the dishes. Pour warm water into the pan to come halfway up the sides of the dishes. Bake in the oven for 35 to 40 minutes, or until the center of each custard still jiggles slightly. Remove from the oven and lift the dishes from the hot water. Let cool briefly, then refrigerate for at least 2 hours or up to 1 day.

When ready to serve, place the dishes on a baking sheet and evenly sprinkle 1 tablespoon sugar over each custard. Using a hand-held blowtorch, caramelize the sugar (see page 11). Garnish the top of each dish with the reserved berries.

Honey-Tangerine Crème Brûlée

Tangerine sections explode with juiciness at the base of this honey custard. Top with a small scoopful of ice cream for a frosty embellishment.

SERVES 6

6 large egg yolks

⅓ cup honey

2 cups heavy (whipping) cream

¼ teaspoon ground cardamom

3 tablespoons curaçao, Triple Sec, or Grand Marnier

4 tangerines (about 1 pound), peeled and sectioned

6 tablespoons sugar for topping

½ pint vanilla or toasted almond ice cream or orange sorbet (optional)

Preheat the oven to 275°F. In a medium bowl, whisk the egg yolks until pale in color. Whisk in the honey, cream, cardamom, and orange liqueur.

Place six standard-size flan dishes in a baking pan. Divide the tangerine sections among the dishes and fill with the custard mixture. Pour warm water into the pan to come halfway up the sides of the dishes. Bake in the oven for 35 to 40 minutes, or until the center of each custard still jiggles slightly. Remove from the oven and lift the dishes from the hot water. Let cool briefly, then refrigerate for 2 hours to chill thoroughly or up to 2 days.

When ready to serve, place the dishes on a baking sheet and evenly sprinkle 1 tablespoon sugar over each custard. Using a hand-held blowtorch, caramelize the sugar (see page 11). Serve with a scoopful of ice cream or sorbet, if desired.

Apple-Calvados Crème Brûlée

Cinnamon-spiced caramelized apples are the base for this brandy-scented custard. A good apple variety to use is the Granny Smith, with its tart-sweet flavor. It keeps its shape nicely after sautéing. Calvados, the apple-infused brandy, lends a nice spark to the dessert.

SERVES 6

2 tablespoons unsalted butter

3 large Granny Smith apples (about 1½ pounds), peeled, cored, and sliced

2 tablespoons plus ⅓ cup granulated sugar

½ teaspoon ground cinnamon

6 large egg yolks

2 cups heavy (whipping) cream

2 tablespoons Calvados or Cognac

6 tablespoons oven-dried brown sugar (see page 11) for topping

Preheat the oven to 275°F. In a large skillet, melt the butter over medium heat, add the apples, and sprinkle with the 2 tablespoons granulated sugar and the cinnamon. Sauté until the apples are soft and lightly caramelized, about 10 minutes.

In a medium bowl, whisk the egg yolks until pale in color, add the remaining ⅓ cup granulated sugar and whisk until dissolved. Gradually whisk in the cream and blend in the Calvados or Cognac.

Place six standard-size flan dishes in a baking pan. Distribute the sautéed apples and then the custard mixture among the dishes. Pour warm water into the pan to come halfway up the sides of the dishes. Bake in the oven for 35 to 40 minutes, or until the center of each custard still jiggles slightly. Remove from the oven and lift the dishes from the hot water. Let cool briefly, then refrigerate for at least 2 hours or up to 2 days.

When ready to serve, place the dishes on a baking sheet and evenly sprinkle 1 tablespoon brown sugar over each custard. Using a hand-held blowtorch, caramelize the sugar (see page 11).

Spicy Persimmon Crème Brûlée

During the holiday season, this is a novel way to enjoy luscious Hachiya persimmons for dessert. You can freeze soft, ripe persimmons whole, with skin on. Dip the fruit in a bowl of warm water and the skin will peel off readily. The sweet heat of ginger is wonderful here.

SERVES 6

6 large egg yolks

⅓ cup firmly packed brown sugar

¾ cup puréed fresh persimmon pulp

1½ cups heavy (whipping) cream

¾ teaspoon ground cinnamon

2 tablespoons finely chopped crystallized ginger

6 tablespoons oven-dried brown sugar (see page 11) for topping

Preheat the oven to 275°F. In a medium bowl, whisk the egg yolks until pale in color and whisk in the ⅓ cup brown sugar until dissolved. Whisk in the persimmon pulp, cream, cinnamon, and crystallized ginger.

Place six standard-size flan dishes in a baking pan. Divide the custard mixture among the dishes. Pour warm water into the pan to come halfway up the sides of the dishes. Bake in the oven for 35 to 40 minutes, or until the center of each custard still jiggles slightly. Remove from the oven and lift the dishes from the hot water. Let cool briefly, then refrigerate for at least 2 hours or up to 2 days.

When ready to serve, place the dishes on a baking sheet and evenly sprinkle 1 tablespoon oven-dried brown sugar over each custard. Using a hand-held blowtorch, caramelize the sugar (see page 11).

Peach and Champagne Sabayon Crème Brûlée

Champagne is used to poach the peaches and as the base of the frothy custard filling. Or, use a dessert wine, such as a Malvasia Blanca or Moscato d'Oro. Top with Cognac-flavored whipped cream for an elegant, cool flourish.

SERVES 6

2 large peaches, peeled, pitted, and sliced

1½ cups sec (slightly sweet) champagne or dessert wine

6 large egg yolks

⅓ cup granulated sugar

1 teaspoon grated lemon zest

1 cup heavy (whipping) cream

1 tablespoon confectioners' sugar, plus 6 tablespoons for topping

2 tablespoons Cognac

In a medium saucepan, combine the peaches and 1 cup of the champagne or wine. Bring to a simmer over medium heat and cook, uncovered, for 5 minutes, or until tender, letting the juices reduce until almost evaporated. Remove from the heat and let cool.

In the top of a double boiler, whisk the egg yolks until pale in color. Whisk in the granulated sugar until dissolved. Whisk in the lemon zest. Place over simmering water and whisk until the yolks are light and foamy, about 5 minutes. Gradually whisk in the remaining ½ cup champagne and ½ cup of the cream. Using a hand-held electric mixer, beat until the mixture is thick, light, and tripled in volume, about 15 minutes. Let cool, then refrigerate for 30 minutes.

In a deep bowl, whip the remaining ½ cup cream until soft peaks form. Blend in the 1 tablespoon confectioners' sugar and the Cognac.

When ready to serve, reserve half of the peach slices for topping. Divide the remaining peach slices among six standard-size flan dishes. Spoon the custard over and top with the remaining peach slices. Place the dishes on a baking sheet and, using a small sieve, evenly sprinkle 1 tablespoon confectioners' sugar over each custard. Using a hand-held blowtorch, caramelize the sugar (see page 11). Garnish with the flavored whipped cream.

Pineapple-Macadamia Crème Brûlée

This is a quick, last-minute dessert, ideal for impromptu dinners. Luscious pineapple chunks and crunchy macadamia nuts underlie the creamy layer and caramelized sugar topping. An enzyme in fresh pineapple prevents an egg custard from setting during baking, so this is a delicious way to integrate this fruit for a spur-of-the-moment dessert.

SERVES 6

1 pineapple, peeled, cored, and diced

6 tablespoons chopped macadamia nuts or roasted cashew nuts

¾ cup sour cream or crème fraîche

6 tablespoons raw or demerara sugar for topping

Mint sprigs or edible flowers for garnish

Place six standard-size flan dishes in a baking pan and divide the pineapple among them. Sprinkle with the nuts. Top with the sour cream or crème fraîche, spreading it evenly. Evenly sprinkle 1 tablespoon raw or demerara sugar over each dessert.

Using a hand-held blowtorch, caramelize the sugar (see page 11). Garnish with a sprig of mint or an edible flower.

No-Bake Zesty Lime Crème Brûlée

This no-bake brûlée does not require egg yolks, as the cream is thickened with lime juice. It is wonderfully refreshing, and may be served in small tart shells instead of dishes.

SERVES 6

2 ¼ cups heavy (whipping) cream

½ cup granulated sugar

1 tablespoon grated lime zest

⅓ cup freshly squeezed lime juice

6 tablespoons oven-dried brown sugar (see page 11) or confectioners' sugar for topping

In a medium saucepan, combine the cream and granulated sugar. Cook over medium heat, stirring constantly, until the sugar dissolves and the mixture comes to a gentle simmer. Cook for 2 minutes more. Remove from the heat and stir in the lime zest. Gradually stir in the lime juice.

Place six standard-size flan dishes in a baking pan. Divide the custard mixture among the dishes. Refrigerate for at least 2 hours or up to 2 days.

When ready to serve, place the dishes on a baking sheet and evenly sprinkle 1 tablespoon brown or confectioners' sugar over each custard. (If using confectioners' sugar, use a small sieve to sprinkle the sugar.) Using a hand-held blowtorch, caramelize the sugar (see page 11).

Bananas Foster Crème Brûlée

As the sugar topping caramelizes, banana slices warm and sweeten on this rum-scented custard. Bananas Foster, made with caramelized bananas, is a favorite in the South, where Lucy Foster created it.

SERVES 6

6 large egg yolks

⅓ cup granulated sugar

2 cups heavy (whipping) cream

2 teaspoons grated orange zest

3 tablespoons dark rum or
   1 teaspoon vanilla extract

2 large bananas

6 tablespoons oven-dried brown
   sugar (see page 11) or turbinado
   sugar for topping

Preheat the oven to 275 °F. In a medium bowl, whisk the egg yolks until pale in color. Whisk in the granulated sugar until dissolved. Gradually whisk in the cream, then blend in the orange zest and rum or vanilla extract.

Place six standard-size flan dishes in a baking pan. Divide the custard mixture among the dishes. Pour warm water into the pan to come halfway up the sides of the dishes. Bake in the oven for 35 to 40 minutes, or until the center of each custard still jiggles slightly. Remove from the oven and lift the dishes from the hot water. Let cool briefly, then refrigerate for at least 2 hours or up to 2 days.

When ready to serve, place the dishes on a baking sheet. Slice the bananas thinly and overlap them over the top of each custard. Evenly sprinkle 1 tablespoon brown or turbinado sugar over each custard. Using a hand-held blowtorch, caramelize the sugar (see page 11).

Raspberry-Framboise Crème Brûlée

Fresh raspberries ornament this silken custard and add a flavor contrast. Flan dishes allow for an ample sugar crust to garnish with raspberries and chocolate sorbet.

SERVES 6

2 cups fresh raspberries

6 large egg yolks

⅓ cup granulated sugar

½ cup crème fraîche

1½ cups heavy (whipping) cream

3 tablespoons framboise

1 tablespoon grated lemon zest

6 tablespoons confectioners' sugar for topping

½ pint chocolate sorbet or vanilla bean ice cream (optional)

Preheat the oven to 275°F. Place six standard-size flan dishes in a baking pan. Reserve ½ cup of the raspberries for garnish. Divide the remaining raspberries among the dishes.

In a medium bowl, whisk the egg yolks until pale in color, then whisk in the granulated sugar until dissolved. Whisk in the crème fraîche, heavy cream, framboise, and lemon zest.

Divide the custard mixture among the dishes. Pour warm water into the pan to come halfway up the sides of the dishes. Bake in the oven for 35 to 40 minutes, or until the center of each custard still jiggles slightly. Remove from the oven and lift the dishes from the hot water. Let cool briefly, then refrigerate for at least 2 hours or up to 1 day.

When ready to serve, place the dishes on a baking sheet and, using a small sieve, evenly sprinkle 1 tablespoon confectioners' sugar over each custard. Using a hand-held blowtorch, caramelize the sugar (see page 11). Garnish the tops of the dishes with the reserved raspberries and small scoops of sorbet or ice cream, if desired.

Frangipane-Apricot Crème Brûlée

This triple-layer crème brûlée has an undercoat of crisp almond frangipane, then sweet-tart apricots and satiny custard, topped with a caramelized sugar crust. Any surplus fruit freezes beautifully, halved and pitted, for year-round enjoyment in desserts and morning smoothies.

SERVES 6

½ cup (2½ ounces) blanched whole almonds, toasted (see page 28)

⅔ cup granulated sugar

2 tablespoons egg white

2 tablespoons unsalted butter

1½ pounds apricots, halved, pitted, and quartered

6 large egg yolks

2 cups heavy (whipping) cream

2 tablespoons brandy or Cognac

6 tablespoons oven-dried brown sugar (see page 11) for topping

½ pint toasted almond or vanilla bean ice cream (optional)

Preheat the oven to 275 °F. In a food processor fitted with the steel blade, combine the almonds and ⅓ cup of the granulated sugar. Process until the nuts are finely ground. Add the egg white and butter and pulse until the mixture comes together. Place six standard-size flan dishes in a baking pan. Divide the almond mixture among the dishes. Nestle the apricots on top of the almond mixture.

In a medium bowl, whisk the egg yolks until pale in color. Whisk in the remaining ⅓ cup granulated sugar until dissolved. Gradually whisk in the cream and blend in the brandy or Cognac.

Divide the custard mixture among the dishes. Pour warm water into the pan to come halfway up the sides of the dishes. Bake in the oven for 35 to 40 minutes, or until the center of each custard still jiggles slightly. Remove from the oven and lift the dishes from the hot water. Let cool briefly, then refrigerate for at least 2 hours or up to 2 days.

When ready to serve, place the dishes on a baking sheet and, using a small sieve, evenly sprinkle 1 tablespoon brown sugar over each custard. Using a hand-held blowtorch, caramelize the sugar (see page 11). Garnish with small scoops of ice cream, if desired.

Pear Crème Brûlée

Choose firm, ripe cooking pears such as Anjou or Bosc for this brandy-laced brûlée.

SERVES 6

¾ cup granulated sugar

2 cups heavy (whipping) cream

6 large egg yolks

3 tablespoons Poire William
(pear brandy)

2 large, firm Anjou or Bosc pears,
peeled, halved, and cored

¼ teaspoon freshly grated nutmeg

6 tablespoons oven-dried brown
sugar (see page 11) or confectioners' sugar for topping

Whipped cream flavored with
Poire William for garnish

Preheat the oven to 275 °F. Place six standard-size flan dishes in a baking pan. Put the granulated sugar in a small, heavy saucepan and heat over medium-high heat, shaking the pan until the sugar caramelizes. Immediately pour about 1½ tablespoons caramel into each of the dishes, leaving about 6 tablespoons caramel remaining in the pan. Carefully pour the cream into the saucepan with the caramel (it will sputter), and heat, stirring until the caramel is dissolved. Remove from the heat and let cool to room temperature.

In a medium bowl, whisk the egg yolks until pale in color. Whisk in the caramel cream. Stir in the pear brandy.

Cut the pears into slices and divide them among the dishes. Dust with nutmeg, then divide the custard mixture among the dishes. Pour warm water into the pan to come halfway up the sides of the dishes. Bake in the oven for 35 to 40 minutes, or until the center of each custard still jiggles slightly. Remove from the oven and lift the dishes from the hot water. Let cool briefly, then refrigerate for at least 2 hours or up to 2 days.

When ready to serve, place the dishes on a baking sheet and evenly sprinkle 1 tablespoon brown sugar or confectioners' sugar over each custard. (If using confectioners' sugar, use a small sieve to sprinkle the sugar.) Using a hand-held blowtorch, caramelize the sugar (see page 11). Garnish with the flavored whipped cream.

CHOCOLATE AND NUTTY

ALL STYLES OF CHOCOLATE—BITTERSWEET, MILK, AND WHITE—AND A variety of nuts—almonds, hazelnuts, pecans, and walnuts—lend an elegant richness or an intriguing crunch to these delectable crèmes brûlées.

Double-Chocolate Crème Brûlée

Chocolate always makes a winning sweet, and this one doubles the bonus with a marbleized duo of bittersweet and white chocolate custard. This eye-catching dessert goes together quickly, as you simply divide the basic egg and cream mixture for each filling.

SERVES 6

2 cups heavy (whipping) cream

6 large egg yolks

⅓ cup sugar, plus 6 tablespoons for topping

1 teaspoon vanilla extract

3 ounces white chocolate, chopped

1 tablespoon brandy

3 ounces bittersweet chocolate, chopped

1 tablespoon Kahlúa

Preheat the oven to 275°F. Pour the cream into a medium saucepan. Place over medium heat until small bubbles form around the edges of the pan. In a medium bowl, whisk the egg yolks until pale in color. Whisk in the ⅓ cup sugar until dissolved. Whisk in the heated cream and vanilla extract. Pour half of the mixture into a large bowl and stir in the white chocolate until it melts; blend in the brandy. Stir the chopped bittersweet chocolate into the remaining mixture until melted. Blend in the Kahlúa.

Place six standard-size flan dishes in a baking pan. Divide the white chocolate mixture among the dishes. Let cool, then refrigerate for 30 minutes to cool and set. Refrigerate the bowl of bittersweet chocolate custard at the same time.

Remove the dishes from the refrigerator. Spoon dollops of the bittersweet chocolate custard on the white chocolate custard, and with a fork, swirl it to form a marbleized pattern.

Pour warm water into the pan to come halfway up the sides of the dishes. Bake in the oven for 35 to 40 minutes, or until the center of each custard still jiggles slightly. Remove from the oven and lift the dishes from the hot water. Let cool briefly, then refrigerate for at least 2 hours or up to 2 days.

When ready to serve, place the dishes on a baking sheet and evenly sprinkle 1 tablespoon sugar over each custard. Using a hand-held blowtorch, caramelize the sugar (see page 11).

Gianduia Crème Brûlée

Gianduia—the addictive Italian duo of hazelnuts and chocolate—is a winning flavor in this custard. A commercial hazelnut-cocoa paste emphasizes the nutty taste in chocolate cream, and toasted hazelnuts embellish the caramelized sugar topping.

SERVES 6

6 tablespoons hazelnuts, toasted and skinned (see note)

2 cups heavy (whipping) cream

⅓ cup hazelnut-cocoa paste, such as Nutella

4 ounces semisweet or bitter-sweet chocolate, chopped

6 large egg yolks

⅓ cup sugar, plus 6 tablespoons for topping

Preheat the oven to 275°F. Finely chop the hazelnuts.

Pour the cream into a medium saucepan. Place over medium heat until small bubbles form around the edges of the pan. Remove from the heat and stir in the hazelnut-cocoa paste and chocolate until blended; let cool to room temperature.

In a medium bowl, whisk the egg yolks until pale in color. Whisk in the ⅓ cup sugar until dissolved. Whisk in the chocolate cream.

Place six standard-size flan dishes in a baking pan. Divide the custard mixture among the dishes. Sprinkle with the toasted nuts. Pour warm water into the pan to come halfway up the sides of the dishes. Bake in the oven for 35 to 40 minutes, or until the center of each custard still jiggles slightly. Remove from the oven and lift the dishes from the hot water. Let cool 10 minutes, then refrigerate for at least 2 hours or up to 2 days.

When ready to serve, place the dishes on a baking sheet. Evenly sprinkle 1 tablespoon sugar over the top of each custard. Using a hand-held blowtorch, caramelize the sugar (see page 11).

Toasting and Skinning Hazelnuts: Preheat the oven to 325°F. Place the nuts on a baking sheet and bake in the oven for 8 to 10 minutes, or until lightly toasted. Remove from the oven, wrap in a tea towel, and rub to remove most of the papery skins.

Mexican Chocolate Crème Brûlée

Dip into this luscious chocolate brûlée to discover a cinnamon syrup under the custard. Mexican chocolate is a bittersweet chocolate with cinnamon, vanilla, sugar, and often ground almonds added; look for the Ibarra brand. Piloncillo, a cone-shaped dark brown sugar with a delicious molasses overtone, is available in Latin markets. Shave it with a chef's knife.

SERVES 6

2 cups heavy (whipping) cream

1 cinnamon stick

5 ounces Mexican chocolate or bittersweet chocolate, chopped

CINNAMON SYRUP:
3 tablespoons packed dark brown sugar

3 tablespoons light corn syrup

1½ teaspoons ground cinnamon

2 teaspoons unsalted butter

3 tablespoons half-and-half

5 large egg yolks

⅓ cup granulated sugar

1 teaspoon vanilla extract

6 tablespoons shaved piloncillo or oven-dried brown sugar (see page 11) for topping

Whipped cream for garnish (optional)

Preheat the oven to 275 °F. Pour the cream into a medium saucepan, add the cinnamon stick, and place over medium heat until small bubbles form around the edges of the pan. Add the chocolate and stir until blended. Remove from the heat and let cool to room temperature. Remove the cinnamon stick.

Meanwhile, make the cinnamon syrup: In a small saucepan, combine the dark brown sugar, corn syrup, and cinnamon. Bring to a boil over medium heat and boil for 1 minute. Remove from the heat and stir in the butter and half-and-half. Place six standard-size flan dishes in a baking pan. Divide the syrup among the dishes.

In a medium bowl, whisk the egg yolks until pale in color. Whisk in the granulated sugar until dissolved. Whisk in the chocolate cream and vanilla extract.

Divide the custard mixture among the dishes (atop the syrup). Pour warm water into the pan to come halfway up the sides of the dishes. Bake in the oven for 35 to 40 minutes, or until the center of each custard still jiggles slightly. Remove from the oven and lift the dishes from the hot water. Let cool briefly, then refrigerate for at least 2 hours or up to 2 days.

When ready to serve, place the dishes on a baking sheet. Evenly sprinkle 1 tablespoon piloncillo or oven-dried brown sugar over the top of each custard. Using a hand-held blowtorch, caramelize the sugar (see page 11). Top with whipped cream, if desired.

White Chocolate–Cognac Crème Brûlée

Shreds of bittersweet chocolate fleck this luscious, creamy white chocolate dessert. It is fun to adorn the top with long curls of bittersweet chocolate.

SERVES 6

2 cups heavy (whipping) cream

6 ounces white chocolate, chopped

6 large egg yolks

⅓ cup sugar, plus 6 tablespoons for topping

3 tablespoons Cognac

2 ounces bittersweet chocolate, chopped, or ⅔ cup semisweet chocolate chips, plus chocolate curls for garnish (see note)

Preheat the oven to 275 °F. Pour the cream into a medium saucepan. Place over medium heat until small bubbles form around the edges of the pan. Remove from the heat and stir in the white chocolate until blended. Let cool to room temperature.

In a medium bowl, whisk the egg yolks until pale in color. Whisk in the ⅓ cup sugar until dissolved. Whisk in the white chocolate cream and Cognac.

Place six standard-size flan dishes in a baking pan. Sprinkle half of the chopped bittersweet chocolate or semisweet chocolate chips in the bottom of the dishes. Divide the custard mixture among the dishes. Sprinkle the remaining chocolate on top. Pour warm water into the pan to come halfway up the sides of the dishes. Bake in the oven for 35 to 40 minutes, or until the center of each custard still jiggles slightly. Remove from the oven and lift the dishes from the hot water. Let cool briefly, then refrigerate for at least 2 hours or up to 2 days.

When ready to serve, place the dishes on a baking sheet and evenly sprinkle 1 tablespoon sugar over the top of each custard. Using a hand-held blowtorch, caramelize the sugar (see page 11). Garnish with chocolate curls.

Making Chocolate Curls: Let a bar of bittersweet chocolate warm to room temperature or slightly warmer. Using a vegetable peeler, peel long curls from the bar.

Chocolate Rum Macaroon Crème Brûlée

For a nice surprise, rum-soaked amaretti cookies or macaroons support the rich chocolate filling of this dessert, creating a delectable biteful.

SERVES 6

18 small amaretti cookies or
  macaroons

¼ cup dark rum or brandy

2 cups heavy (whipping) cream

5 ounces bittersweet chocolate,
  chopped

5 large egg yolks

⅓ cup granulated sugar

1 teaspoon vanilla extract

6 tablespoons oven-dried light
  brown sugar (see page 11) for
  topping

Preheat the oven to 275 °F. Place six standard-size flan dishes in a baking pan. Arrange the cookies in the bottom of the dishes and drizzle with the rum or brandy.

Pour the cream into a medium saucepan. Place over medium heat until small bubbles form around the edges of the pan. Remove from the heat and stir in the chocolate until blended; let cool to room temperature.

In a medium bowl, whisk the egg yolks until pale in color. Whisk in the granulated sugar until dissolved. Whisk in the chocolate cream and vanilla extract.

Divide the custard mixture among the dishes. Pour warm water into the pan to come halfway up the sides of the dishes. Bake in the oven for 35 to 40 minutes, or until the center of each custard still jiggles slightly. Remove from the oven and lift the dishes from the hot water. Let cool briefly, then refrigerate for at least 2 hours or up to 2 days.

When ready to serve, place the dishes on a baking sheet. Evenly sprinkle 1 tablespoon brown sugar over the top of each custard. Using a hand-held blowtorch, caramelize the sugar (see page 11).

Kona–Milk Chocolate Crème Brûlée

Swirls of milk chocolate ripple this robust coffee brûlée. For coffee-lovers, this combines a sumptuous beverage and dessert in a bowl.

SERVES 6

6 teaspoons instant espresso or instant coffee granules

3 tablespoons hot water

2 cups heavy (whipping) cream

6 large egg yolks

⅓ cup firmly packed light brown sugar

3 tablespoons brandy or Cognac

¾ cup milk chocolate or semi-sweet chocolate chips or 4½ ounces bittersweet chocolate, chopped

6 tablespoons turbinado sugar for topping

Preheat the oven to 275 °F. In a medium bowl, dissolve the espresso or coffee granules in the hot water and stir in the cream.

In another medium bowl, whisk the egg yolks until pale in color. Whisk in the brown sugar until dissolved. Whisk in the espresso mixture and brandy or Cognac.

Place six standard-size flan dishes in a baking pan. Scatter half the chocolate in the bottom of the dishes. Divide the custard mixture among the dishes. Scatter the remaining chocolate over the top. Pour warm water into the pan to come halfway up the sides of the dishes. Bake in the oven for 35 to 40 minutes, or until the center of each custard still jiggles slightly. Remove from the oven and lift the dishes from the hot water. Let cool briefly, then refrigerate for at least 2 hours or up to 2 days.

When ready to serve, place the dishes on a baking sheet and evenly sprinkle 1 tablespoon turbinado sugar over each custard. Using a hand-held blowtorch, caramelize the sugar (see page 11).

Ice Cream Crème Brûlée

The presentation is dazzling, yet the assembly is quite easy for this stellar sweet. A fluted chocolate dish holds an ice cream ball topped by an almond-coated caramel disk. Choose your favorite ice cream or make your own. Fresh berries, such as raspberries, blueberries, or blackberries, make a delightful optional garnish.

SERVES 6

6 tablespoons turbinado sugar

6 tablespoons toasted almonds (see page 28), finely chopped

4 ounces bittersweet chocolate, chopped

1 teaspoon vegetable oil, plus more for brushing

1½ pints vanilla, coffee, or chocolate bean ice cream

Fresh raspberries, blueberries, or blackberries for garnish (optional)

Line a baking sheet with aluminum foil. Place a 4-inch-diameter bowl upside down on the foil and draw around it; repeat to make 6 circles. Brush with vegetable oil. Evenly sprinkle each circle with 1 tablespoon sugar, covering completely. Using a hand-held blowtorch, caramelize the sugar (see page 11). Immediately sprinkle with the almonds; let cool for a few minutes, then carefully peel the caramel disks from the foil and set aside.

Place 6 fluted cupcake papers in a muffin pan. In a large stainless steel bowl, combine the chocolate and the 1 teaspoon vegetable oil. Place the bowl over a saucepan with 1 inch of simmering water, stirring until the chocolate melts. With a small spatula, spread the chocolate in a thin coating on the bottom and sides of each paper. Place in the freezer for 15 to 20 minutes to set. Carefully peel the paper from the chocolate cups and refrigerate the cups until serving time.

To serve, place each chocolate cup on a dessert plate. Scoop the ice cream into 6 large round balls and place one in each of the chocolate cups. Scatter over a few berries, if desired. Arrange a caramel disk on top of each cup at a slight angle. Serve at once.

Amaretto-Espresso Crème Brûlée

The pairing of coffee and almonds is a winning duo here. The almond flavor gets a boost from the caramelized nut topping.

SERVES 6

4 teaspoons instant espresso or
    instant coffee granules

2 tablespoons hot water

2 cups heavy (whipping) cream

6 large egg yolks

⅓ cup firmly packed light
    brown sugar

4 tablespoons amaretto or Kahlúa

6 tablespoons sliced almonds

6 tablespoons oven-dried brown
    sugar (see page 11) for topping

Preheat the oven to 275 °F. In a medium bowl, dissolve the espresso or coffee granules in the hot water and stir in the cream.

    In a medium bowl, whisk the egg yolks until pale in color. Add the ⅓ cup light brown sugar and whisk until dissolved. Whisk in the espresso mixture and the amaretto or Kahlùa.

    Place six standard-size flan dishes in a baking pan. Divide the custard mixture among the dishes. Pour warm water into the pan to come halfway up the sides of the dishes. Bake in the oven for 35 to 40 minutes, or until the center of each custard still jiggles slightly. Remove from the oven and lift the dishes from the hot water. Let cool briefly, then refrigerate for at least 2 hours or up to 2 days.

    When ready to serve, place the dishes on a baking sheet. Scatter the almonds over the top of each dish. Evenly sprinkle 1 tablespoon oven-dried brown sugar over each custard. Using a hand-held blowtorch, caramelize the sugar (see page 11).

Maple-Walnut Crème Brûlée

Maple sugar in the topping and maple syrup in the custard give a lovely pronounced sweetness to this walnut-enhanced dessert.

SERVES 6

⅔ cup walnut halves, toasted (see page 28)

6 large egg yolks

⅓ cup maple syrup

2 cups heavy (whipping) cream

6 tablespoons maple sugar for topping

Reserve 12 walnut halves for the topping and chop the remainder. Preheat the oven to 275 °F.

In a medium bowl, whisk the egg yolks until pale in color. Whisk in the maple syrup and cream.

Place six standard-size flan dishes in a baking pan. Divide the custard mixture among the dishes. Sprinkle with the chopped walnuts and place 2 halves in the center of each dish. Pour warm water into the pan to come halfway up the sides of the dishes. Bake in the oven for 35 to 40 minutes, or until the center of each custard still jiggles slightly. Remove from the oven and lift the dishes from the hot water. Let cool briefly, then refrigerate for at least 2 hours or up to 2 days.

When ready to serve, place the dishes on a baking sheet. Evenly sprinkle 1 tablespoon maple sugar over each custard. Using a hand-held blowtorch, caramelize the sugar (see page 11).

Butterscotch-Pecan Crème Brûlée

Butterscotch candies lace this brûlée with sweet nuggets, while melted butterscotch chips enhance the custard. The pecans contribute both a superb crunch and a decorative design to the topping.

SERVES 6

¾ cup pecan halves, toasted
  (see page 28)

2 cups heavy (whipping) cream

¾ cup butterscotch chips

6 large egg yolks

2 tablespoons brandy or
  1 teaspoon vanilla extract

6 tablespoons oven-dried brown
  sugar (see page 11) for topping

Reserve 18 pecan halves for the topping and finely chop the remainder. Preheat the oven to 275 °F.

Pour the cream into a medium saucepan. Place over medium heat until small bubbles form around the edges of the pan. Remove from the heat and stir in ½ cup of the butterscotch chips until melted. Set aside and let cool to room temperature.

In a medium bowl, whisk the egg yolks until pale in color. Whisk in the butterscotch cream and brandy or vanilla extract.

Place six standard-size flan dishes in a baking pan. Divide the custard mixture among the dishes. Scatter the remaining ¼ cup butterscotch chips and chopped pecans over the top of the dishes. Place 3 of the pecan halves in a star pattern on top of each dish. Pour warm water into the pan to come halfway up the sides of the dishes. Bake in the oven for 35 to 40 minutes, or until the center of each custard still jiggles slightly. Remove from the oven and lift the dishes from the hot water. Let cool briefly, then refrigerate for at least 2 hours or up to 2 days.

When ready to serve, place the dishes on a baking sheet. Evenly sprinkle 1 tablespoon sugar over each custard. Using a hand-held blowtorch, caramelize the sugar (see page 11).

Hazelnut Crème Brûlée

Hazelnuts scent the creamy custard and the caramelized crust in this delectable dessert. Pair with a shower of raspberries or blueberries for a refreshing finish, if you wish.

SERVES 6

⅔ cup hazelnuts, toasted and skinned (see page 59)

2 cups heavy (whipping) cream

6 large egg yolks

⅓ cup sugar, plus 6 tablespoons for topping

3 tablespoons Frangelico or brandy

½ cup fresh raspberries or blueberries for garnish (optional)

Place ⅓ cup of the hazelnuts in a food processor or blender and process until finely ground. Finely chop the remaining nuts and set aside.

Preheat the oven to 275 °F. In a medium saucepan, combine the cream and ground nuts. Place over medium heat until small bubbles form around the edges of the pan. Remove from the heat and let cool to room temperature.

In a medium bowl, whisk the egg yolks until pale in color. Whisk in the ⅓ cup sugar until dissolved. Whisk in the hazelnut cream and Frangelico or brandy.

Place six standard-size flan dishes in a baking pan. Divide the custard mixture among the dishes. Sprinkle with the chopped nuts. Pour warm water into the pan to come halfway up the sides of the dishes. Bake in the oven for 35 to 40 minutes, or until the center of each custard still jiggles slightly. Remove from the oven and lift the dishes from the hot water. Let cool briefly, then refrigerate for at least 2 hours or up to 2 days.

When ready to serve, place the dishes on a baking sheet. Evenly sprinkle 1 tablespoon sugar over each custard. Using a hand-held blowtorch, caramelize the sugar (see page 11). Garnish with a few raspberries or blueberries, if desired.

Toffee Crème Brûlée

Chocolate toffee nuggets embellish this dessert for a candylike treat. Use a top-quality commercial toffee and chop it coarsely.

SERVES 6

6 large egg yolks

⅓ cup granulated sugar

2 cups heavy (whipping) cream

2 tablespoons Cognac or
   1 teaspoon vanilla extract

6 ounces chocolate-covered
   toffee, coarsely chopped

6 tablespoons oven-dried brown
   sugar (see page 11) or raw sugar
   for topping

Preheat the oven to 275 °F. In a medium bowl, whisk the egg yolks until pale in color. Whisk in the granulated sugar until dissolved. Whisk in the cream and Cognac or vanilla extract.

Place six standard-size flan dishes in a baking pan. Divide the toffee evenly among the dishes. Divide the custard mixture among the dishes. Pour warm water into the pan to come halfway up the sides of the dishes. Bake in the oven for 35 to 40 minutes, or until the center of each custard still jiggles slightly. Remove from the oven and lift the dishes from the hot water. Let cool briefly, then refrigerate for at least 2 hours or up to 2 days.

When ready to serve, place the dishes on a baking sheet and evenly sprinkle 1 tablespoon brown or raw sugar over each custard. Using a hand-held blow-torch, caramelize the sugar (see page 11).

Peanut Butter Crème Brûlée

This is for all lovers of peanut butter. Other nut butters, such as almond and cashew, are excellent here as well. Match them with the appropriate chopped nuts.

SERVES 6

2 cups heavy (whipping) cream

6 tablespoons peanut butter

6 large egg yolks

⅓ cup firmly packed light brown sugar

1 teaspoon vanilla extract

6 tablespoons finely chopped roasted peanuts

6 tablespoons oven-dried brown sugar (see page 11) for topping

Preheat the oven to 275°F. Pour the cream into a medium saucepan. Place over medium heat until small bubbles form around the edges of the pan. Stir in the peanut butter until blended. Remove from the heat and let cool to room temperature.

In a medium bowl, whisk the egg yolks until pale in color. Whisk in the light brown sugar until dissolved. Whisk in the nut-flavored cream and vanilla extract.

Place six standard-size flan dishes in a baking pan. Divide the custard mixture among the dishes. Pour warm water into the pan to come halfway up the sides of the dishes. Bake in the oven for 35 to 40 minutes, or until the center of each custard still jiggles slightly. Remove from the oven and lift the dishes from the hot water. Let cool briefly, then refrigerate for 2 hours or up to 2 days.

When ready to serve, place the dishes on a baking sheet. Sprinkle with the chopped nuts. Evenly sprinkle 1 tablespoon oven-dried brown sugar over the top of each custard. Using a hand-held blowtorch, caramelize the sugar (see page 11).

SAVORY

BESIDES THE BELOVED SWEET DESSERT BRÛLÉES, THERE IS A place for savory versions. These are ideal as a first course, a side dish, or a light entrée for brunch, lunch, or dinner. Or, some may serve a versatile position in all three culinary situations. You can assemble savory crèmes brûlées early in the day and refrigerate, ready for last-minute baking. They make a delightful treat for guest occasions.

Mushroom and Goat Cheese Crème Brûlée

Creamy goat cheese and woodsy mushrooms are paired in this enticing dish. Portobellos or brown cremini mushrooms are good choices here.

SERVES 6

1 tablespoon unsalted butter

1 tablespoon extra-virgin olive oil

1 pound portobello or cremini mushrooms, thinly sliced and cut into 1-inch pieces if larger

5 large egg yolks

1 cup heavy (whipping) cream

½ cup half-and-half

1 tablespoon minced fresh tarragon or thyme or ¾ teaspoon dried tarragon or thyme

3 tablespoons minced fresh chives

¼ teaspoon salt

Freshly ground black pepper to taste

4 ounces mild goat cheese, sliced

½ cup (2 ounces) shredded Gruyère cheese

24 teaspoons grated Parmesan cheese for topping

Preheat the oven to 275 °F. In a medium saucepan, melt the butter with the olive oil over medium-high heat. Add the mushrooms and sauté for 1 to 2 minutes, or until glazed.

In a medium bowl, whisk the egg yolks until pale in color. Whisk in the cream, half-and-half, tarragon or thyme, chives, salt, and pepper.

Place six standard-size flan dishes in a baking pan. Divide the mushrooms and goat cheese among the dishes. Divide the custard mixture among the dishes. Sprinkle with the Gruyère cheese. Pour warm water into the pan to come halfway up the sides of the dishes. Bake in the oven for 35 to 40 minutes, or until the center of each custard still jiggles slightly. Remove from the oven and lift the dishes from the hot water. Place the dishes on a baking sheet.

Evenly sprinkle 4 teaspoons Parmesan cheese over each of the custards. Using a hand-held blowtorch, brown the cheese (see page 11). Serve hot.

Gorgonzola and Leek Crème Brûlée

This savory custard features creamy Gorgonzola and the sweet succulence of leeks. Let it precede an entrée of barbecued steak or duck breast for a guest dinner. You can assemble it in advance and bake at the last minute, or bake it ahead and reheat to serve. Finish the dishes with Parmesan cheese for a sharp bite, or sugar for a sweet touch.

SERVES 6

1 tablespoon extra-virgin olive oil

2 medium-large leeks (about 12 ounces total), split lengthwise, washed thoroughly, and sliced crosswise

1 small yellow onion, chopped

5 large egg yolks

1 cup heavy (whipping) cream

1 cup half-and-half

5 ounces Gorgonzola cheese, crumbled

1 tablespoon minced fresh dill or tarragon or ¾ teaspoon dried dill or tarragon

3 tablespoons minced fresh Italian parsley

Salt and freshly ground black pepper to taste

24 teaspoons grated Parmesan cheese or 9 teaspoons sugar for topping

Preheat the oven to 275 °F. In a medium saucepan, heat the olive oil over medium heat. Add the leeks and onion and sauté for 7 to 10 minutes, or until soft.

In a medium bowl, whisk the egg yolks until pale in color. Whisk in the cream and half-and-half. Mix in the leeks, onions, Gorgonzola cheese, dill or tarragon, parsley, and salt and pepper.

Place six standard-size flan dishes in a baking pan. Divide the custard mixture among the dishes. Pour warm water into the pan to come halfway up the sides of the dishes. Bake in the oven for 35 to 40 minutes, or until the center of each custard still jiggles slightly. Remove from the oven and lift the dishes from the hot water. Place the dishes on a baking sheet.

Evenly sprinkle 4 teaspoons Parmesan cheese or 1½ teaspoons sugar over each custard. Using a hand-held blowtorch, brown the cheese or caramelize the sugar (see page 11). Serve hot.

Broccoli and Red Pepper Crème Brûlée

Serve this red and green savory as a side dish with a prime rib roast during the Christmas season. It is especially handsome and easy to serve on a buffet table.

SERVES 6

1 pound broccoli florets, cut into 1-inch pieces

3 tablespoons extra-virgin olive oil

1 red bell pepper, halved, seeded, and diced

2 green onions (including tops), chopped

1 cup (4 ounces) shredded white Cheddar or Havarti cheese

2 large eggs

2 large egg yolks

1 cup heavy (whipping) cream

½ cup half-and-half

½ teaspoon salt

Freshly ground black pepper to taste

1½ cups ⅜-inch sourdough bread cubes

24 teaspoons grated Parmesan cheese for topping

Preheat the oven to 275 °F. In a medium pan, cook the broccoli in boiling salted water until crisp-tender, about 8 minutes, and drain. Add 1 tablespoon of the olive oil to the same pan and heat over medium heat. Sauté the bell pepper and onions until soft, 2 to 3 minutes.

Place six standard-size flan dishes in a baking pan and divide the vegetables among the dishes. Sprinkle with the Cheddar or Havarti cheese.

In a medium bowl, whisk the eggs and egg yolks together until pale in color. Gradually whisk in the cream, half-and-half, salt, and pepper. Divide the custard mixture among the dishes. Toss the bread cubes with the remaining 2 tablespoons olive oil. Scatter over the custard mixture.

Pour warm water into the pan to come halfway up the sides of the dishes. Bake in the oven for 35 to 40 minutes, or until the center of each custard still jiggles slightly. Remove from the oven and lift the dishes from the hot water. Place the dishes on a baking sheet.

Evenly sprinkle 4 teaspoons Parmesan cheese over each custard. Using a hand-held blowtorch, brown the cheese and bread cubes (see page 11). Serve hot.

Brie Croustade Crème Brûlée

Slices of toasted brioche or challah bread, Brie, and prosciutto make an intriguing herb-scented brûlée. To serve as a light entrée, accompany with a green salad accented with a few red seedless grapes or red and gold cherry tomatoes.

SERVES 6

5 large egg yolks

1 cup heavy (whipping) cream

1 cup half-and-half

1 tablespoon minced fresh dill or tarragon or ¾ teaspoon dried dill or tarragon

2 tablespoons minced fresh chives

Salt and freshly ground white pepper to taste

6 thin slices brioche or challah bread, toasted and cut into triangles

5 ounces Brie cheese, cut into 6 vertical slices

2 ounces thinly sliced prosciutto, cut into ½-by-1-inch strips

24 teaspoons grated Parmesan cheese or 9 teaspoons sugar for topping

Preheat the oven to 275°F. In a medium bowl, whisk the egg yolks until pale in color. Gradually whisk in the cream and half-and-half. Mix in the dill or tarragon, chives, and salt and pepper.

Place six standard-size flan dishes in a baking pan. Arrange a piece of toasted bread in the bottom of each dish and 1 along the side. Top with a slice of Brie cheese and a few pieces of prosciutto. Divide the custard mixture among the dishes. Pour warm water into the pan to come halfway up the sides of the dishes. Bake in the oven for 35 to 40 minutes, or until the center of each custard still jiggles slightly. Remove from the oven and lift the dishes from the hot water. Place the dishes on a baking sheet.

Evenly sprinkle 4 teaspoons Parmesan cheese or 1½ teaspoons sugar over each custard. Using a hand-held blowtorch, brown the cheese or caramelize the sugar (see page 11). Serve hot.

Wild Rice and Crab Crème Brûlée

Complement sweet crabmeat with a Caesar salad for a guest lunch or light supper.

SERVES 6

1 tablespoon extra-virgin olive oil

¼ cup minced onion or 2 green
   onions (including tops),
   chopped

½ cup wild rice

1½ cups chicken broth

1 tablespoon unsalted butter

6 ounces fresh lump crabmeat or
   cooked small shrimp

3 tablespoons minced fresh
   chives, plus ⅓ cup

2 large eggs

2 large egg yolks

¾ cup heavy (whipping) cream

¾ cup half-and-half

¾ cup (3 ounces) shredded
   Gruyère or Swiss cheese

½ teaspoon salt

Freshly ground black pepper to
   taste

24 teaspoons grated Parmesan
   cheese for topping

In a small saucepan, heat the olive oil over medium heat and sauté the onion until soft, about 5 minutes. Add the rice and broth, cover, and bring to a boil. Reduce the heat to low and simmer for 1 hour, or until the rice is tender. Remove from the heat and set aside.

Preheat the oven to 275 °F. In a small saucepan, melt the butter over medium heat. Sauté the crab or shrimp for 2 minutes. Sprinkle with the 3 tablespoons chives. Remove from the heat and set aside.

In a medium bowl, whisk the eggs and egg yolks together until pale in color. Whisk in the cream and half-and-half. Stir in the rice, crab or shrimp, the remaining ⅓ cup chives, Gruyère or Swiss cheese, salt, and pepper.

Place six standard-size flan dishes in a baking pan. Divide the custard mixture among the dishes. Pour warm water into the pan to come halfway up the sides of the dishes. Bake in the oven for 35 to 40 minutes, or until the center of each custard still jiggles slightly. Remove from the oven and lift the dishes from the hot water. Place the dishes on a baking sheet.

Evenly sprinkle 4 teaspoons Parmesan cheese over each custard. Using a hand-held blowtorch, brown the cheese (see page 11). Serve hot.

Spinach and Feta Crème Brûlée

The classic Greek team of spinach and feta is a winning combination in this succulent vegetable brûlée. This an ideal side dish for roast lamb or shish kebabs.

SERVES 6

8 ounces fresh baby spinach leaves

5 large egg yolks

1 cup heavy (whipping) cream

½ cup half-and-half

2 green onions (including tops), chopped

3 ounces feta cheese, crumbled

1 tablespoon minced fresh oregano or ¾ teaspoon dried oregano

¼ teaspoon salt

Freshly ground black pepper to taste

1 cup ⅜-inch sourdough bread cubes

2 tablespoons extra-virgin olive oil

24 teaspoons grated Parmesan cheese for topping

Preheat the oven to 275°F. Rinse the spinach under cold water and drain briefly. In a large skillet, cover and cook over medium heat until the spinach is barely wilted, 1 to 2 minutes; drain thoroughly.

In a medium bowl, whisk the egg yolks until pale in color. Gradually whisk in the cream and half-and-half. Mix in the wilted spinach, the onions, feta cheese, oregano, salt, and pepper. In a medium bowl, toss the bread cubes with the olive oil.

Place six standard-size flan dishes in a baking pan. Divide the custard mixture among the dishes. Scatter the bread cubes over the custard mixture. Pour warm water into the pan to come halfway up the sides of the dishes. Bake in the oven for 35 to 40 minutes, or until the center of each custard still jiggles slightly. Remove from the oven and lift the dishes from the hot water. Place the dishes on a baking sheet.

Evenly sprinkle 4 teaspoons Parmesan cheese over each custard. Using a hand-held blowtorch, brown the cheese (see page 11). Serve hot.

Sweet Corn–Roasted Red Pepper Crème Brûlée

The sweetness of roasted red peppers complements tender corn kernels in this savory brûlée, an excellent accompaniment to roast chicken, pork chops, or grilled sausages.

SERVES 6

2 tablespoons unsalted butter

Kernels cut from 2 large ears white corn (about 1½ cups)

½ cup diced bottled roasted red peppers

2 tablespoons minced fresh chives

6 large egg yolks

1½ cups heavy (whipping) cream

½ cup half-and-half

Dash of hot pepper sauce

¼ teaspoon salt

Freshly ground black pepper to taste

1 cup (4 ounces) shredded white Cheddar cheese

6 tablespoons oven-dried brown sugar (see page 11) for topping

Preheat the oven to 275 °F. In a medium saucepan, melt the butter over medium heat, add the corn, cover, and cook for 2 minutes, or until tender. Turn into a medium bowl and stir in the peppers and chives.

In a medium bowl, whisk the egg yolks until pale in color. Whisk in the cream, half-and-half, hot pepper sauce, salt, and pepper.

Place six standard-size flan dishes in a baking pan. Divide the vegetable mixture among the dishes. Sprinkle evenly with the Cheddar cheese. Divide the custard mixture among the dishes. Pour warm water into the pan to come halfway up the sides of the dishes. Bake in the oven for 35 to 40 minutes, or until the center of each custard still jiggles slightly. Remove from the oven and lift the dishes from the hot water. Place the dishes on a baking sheet.

Evenly sprinkle 1 tablespoon sugar over each custard. Using a hand-held blowtorch, caramelize the sugar (see page 11). Serve hot.

Sun-Dried Tomato and Olive Crème Brûlée

This flavorful brûlée is an ideal lunch entrée to serve with a green salad. Or, let it star as a first course for a guest dinner. Sun-sweet dried tomatoes, sliced kalamata olives, and nuggets of feta cheese intermingle with herbs in this savory combination. Prepare it in advance and torch at the last minute for ease in presentation.

SERVES 6

6 large egg yolks

1 cup heavy (whipping) cream

1 cup half-and-half

1 cup oil-packed sun-dried tomatoes, drained and chopped

½ cup pitted kalamata olives, sliced

1 cup (5 ounces) crumbled feta cheese

3 tablespoons minced fresh Italian parsley

2 green onions (including tops), chopped

3 tablespoons minced fresh basil

Freshly ground black pepper to taste

24 teaspoons grated Parmesan cheese for topping

Preheat the oven to 275 °F. In a medium bowl, whisk the egg yolks until pale in color. Whisk in the cream and half-and-half. Stir in the tomatoes, olives, feta cheese, parsley, onions, basil, and pepper.

Place six standard-size flan dishes in a baking pan. Divide the custard mixture among the dishes. Pour warm water into the pan to come halfway up the sides of the dishes. Bake in the oven for 35 to 40 minutes, or until the center of each custard still jiggles slightly. Remove from the oven and lift the dishes from the hot water. Place the dishes on a baking sheet.

Evenly sprinkle 4 teaspoons Parmesan cheese over each custard. Using a hand-held blowtorch, brown the cheese (see page 11). Serve hot.

Shrimp and Tarragon Crème Brûlée

Nuggets of succulent shrimp punctuate this elegant savory custard.

SERVES 6

1 tablespoon unsalted butter

2 green onions (including tops) or shallots, finely chopped

12 ounces medium cooked shrimp, cut into ½-inch pieces

2 tablespoons freshly squeezed lemon juice

2 large eggs

2 large egg yolks

¾ cup heavy (whipping) cream

¾ cup half-and-half or whole milk

¾ cup (3 ounces) shredded Gruyère or Swiss cheese

1 tablespoon minced fresh tarragon or ¾ teaspoon dried tarragon

2 tablespoons minced fresh Italian parsley

2 tablespoons minced fresh chives

¼ teaspoon salt

Freshly ground white pepper to taste

24 teaspoons grated Parmesan cheese for topping

Preheat the oven to 275°F. In a large skillet, melt the butter over medium heat. Add the onions or shallots and sauté until soft, about 2 minutes; add the shrimp and heat through. Sprinkle with the lemon juice. Remove from the heat.

In a medium bowl, whisk the eggs and egg yolks together until pale in color. Whisk in the cream and half-and-half or milk. Stir in the shrimp and onions or shallots, Gruyère or Swiss cheese, tarragon, parsley, chives, salt, and pepper.

Place six standard-size flan dishes in a baking pan. Divide the custard mixture among the dishes. Pour warm water into the pan to come halfway up the sides of the dishes. Bake in the oven for 35 to 40 minutes, or until the center of each custard still jiggles slightly. Remove from the oven and lift the dishes from the hot water. Place the dishes on a baking sheet.

Evenly sprinkle 4 teaspoons Parmesan cheese over each custard. Using a hand-held blowtorch, brown the cheese (see page 11). Serve hot.

Salmon and Basil Crème Brûlée

Fresh herbs enhance salmon in this pretty dish. Accompany with sliced tomatoes with fresh mozzarella cheese, fresh asparagus, and warm, crusty bread.

SERVES 6

12 ounces salmon fillet

⅓ cup dry vermouth or dry white wine

1 tablespoon extra-virgin olive oil

2 green onions (including tops) or shallots, finely chopped

2 large eggs

2 large egg yolks

¾ cup heavy (whipping) cream

¾ cup half-and-half or whole milk

⅓ cup minced fresh basil

2 tablespoons minced fresh Italian parsley

2 tablespoons minced fresh chives

¼ teaspoon salt

Freshly ground black pepper to taste

24 teaspoons grated Parmesan cheese for topping

Preheat the oven to 275°F. Place the salmon in a large skillet with the vermouth or wine, cover, and simmer over medium-low heat for 5 to 6 minutes, or until the salmon barely flakes with a fork. Remove from the heat. In a small saucepan, heat the olive oil over medium heat and sauté the onions or shallots until soft, about 5 minutes. Remove from the heat. Flake the salmon, discarding any skin and bones.

In a medium bowl, whisk the eggs and egg yolks together until pale in color. Whisk in the cream and half-and-half or milk. Stir in the salmon, onions or shallots, basil, parsley, chives, salt, and pepper.

Place six standard-size flan dishes in a baking pan. Divide the custard mixture among the dishes. Pour warm water into the pan to come halfway up the sides of the dishes. Bake in the oven for 35 to 40 minutes, or until the center of each custard still jiggles slightly. Remove from the oven and lift the dishes from the hot water. Place the dishes on a baking sheet.

Evenly sprinkle 4 teaspoons Parmesan cheese over each custard. Using a hand-held blowtorch, brown the cheese (see page 11).

Roasted Garlic and Chive Crème Brûlée

Roasting garlic develops a lovely sweetness to the cloves, which are easy to squeeze from their papery skins. These custards are superb as a side dish for roast chicken, barbecued steak, or hamburgers. Or, serve them as a sensual dip for steamed artichokes. Another time, sprinkle the dishes with caviar at serving time for an inviting first course.

SERVES 6

2 bulbs garlic (½ cup roasted)

1 tablespoon extra-virgin olive oil

6 large egg yolks

1 ½ cups heavy (whipping) cream

½ cup half-and-half

⅓ cup minced fresh chives

1 cup (4 ounces) shredded Swiss cheese

Salt and freshly ground white pepper to taste

24 teaspoons grated Parmesan cheese or 6 tablespoons sugar for topping

Preheat the oven to 375 °F. Cut ⅓ inch from the top of each garlic bulb. Place the bulbs on a small sheet of aluminum foil, cut side up, and drizzle with the olive oil. Bake in the oven for 40 minutes, or until soft. Let cool, then squeeze the garlic from the papery skins into a small bowl.

Reduce the oven temperature to 275 °F. In a medium bowl, whisk the egg yolks until pale in color. Whisk in the cream and half-and-half. Stir in the roasted garlic, chives, Swiss cheese, and salt and pepper.

Place six standard-size flan dishes in a baking pan. Divide the custard mixture among the dishes. Pour warm water into the pan to come halfway up the sides of the dishes. Bake in the oven for 35 to 40 minutes, or until the center of each custard still jiggles slightly. Remove from the oven and lift the dishes from the hot water. Place the dishes on a baking sheet.

Evenly sprinkle 4 teaspoons Parmesan cheese or 1 tablespoon sugar over each custard. Using a hand-held blowtorch, brown the cheese or caramelize the sugar (see page 11). Serve hot.

Roasted Onion–Gruyère Crème Brûlée

Oven-roasting sweet onions with a balsamic vinegar and olive oil coating develops a superb sweet, caramelized flavor to perfume this dish.

SERVES 6

1 large white onion, quartered

2 tablespoons balsamic vinegar

1 tablespoon extra-virgin olive oil

½ cup half-and-half

2 large eggs

2 large egg yolks

¾ cup heavy (whipping) cream

¼ teaspoon salt

Freshly ground white pepper to taste

¼ teaspoon freshly grated nutmeg

¾ cup (3 ounces) shredded Gruyère or Swiss cheese

9 teaspoons oven-dried brown sugar (see page 11) or 24 teaspoons grated Parmesan cheese for topping

Preheat the oven to 400°F. Place the onion on a sheet of aluminum foil in a baking dish. Mix together the vinegar and olive oil and pour over the onion, coating it well. Bake in the oven until soft, 50 minutes to 1 hour. Remove from the oven and let cool slightly. Place in a blender or food processor, add the half-and-half, and process until blended. Add the eggs, egg yolks, cream, salt, pepper, and nutmeg and process until blended. Stir in the Gruyère or Swiss cheese.

Reduce the oven temperature to 275°F. Place six standard-size flan dishes in a baking pan. Divide the custard mixture among the dishes. Pour warm water into the pan to come halfway up the sides of the dishes. Bake in the oven for 35 to 40 minutes, or until the center of each custard still jiggles slightly. Remove from the oven and lift the dishes from the hot water. Place the dishes on a baking sheet.

Evenly sprinkle 1½ teaspoons sugar or 4 teaspoons Parmesan cheese over each custard. Using a hand-held blowtorch, caramelize the sugar or brown the cheese (see page 11). Serve hot.

INDEX

TABLE OF EQUIVALENTS

The exact equivalents in the following tables have been rounded for convenience.

LIQUID/DRY MEASURES

U.S.	METRIC
¼ teaspoon	1.25 milliliters
½ teaspoon	2.5 milliliters
1 teaspoon	5 milliliters
1 tablespoon (3 teaspoons)	15 milliliters
1 fluid ounce (2 tablespoons)	30 milliliters
¼ cup	60 milliliters
⅓ cup	80 milliliters
½ cup	120 milliliters
1 cup	240 milliliters
1 pint (2 cups)	480 milliliters
1 quart (4 cups, 32 ounces)	960 milliliters
1 gallon (4 quarts)	3.84 liters
1 ounce (by weight)	28 grams
1 pound	454 grams
2.2 pounds	1 kilogram

OVEN TEMPERATURE

FAHRENHEIT	CELSIUS	GAS
250	120	½
275	140	1
300	150	2
325	160	3
350	180	4
375	190	5
400	200	6
425	220	7
450	230	8
475	240	9
500	260	10

LENGTH

U.S.	METRIC
⅛ inch	3 millimeters
¼ inch	6 millimeters
½ inch	12 millimeters
1 inch	2.5 centimeters